Grandpa, I Want to Hear Your Story

A Grandfather's Guided Journal To Share His Life & His Love

Jeffrey Mason

You can view and answer the questions in this book at www.hearyourstory.com. Access can be through any computer, tablet, or smartphone.

You also will have the ability to print multiple copies of your responses to give to your entire family. Please note there is a small charge to cover the cost of maintaining the site

"The joy
of grandchildren
is measured
in the
heart."
—Author Unknown

IT'S YOUR BIRTHDAY!

"No cowboy was ever faster on the draw than a grandparent
pulling a baby picture out of a wallet." —Author Unknown

1. What is your birthdate?

   _____

2. What was your full name at birth?

   _____

3. Were you named after a relative or someone else of
   significance?

   _____

   _____

   _____

4. In what city were you born?

   _____

5. Were you born in a hospital? If not, where?

   _____

   _____

6. What were your first words?

   _____

   _____

7. How old were your parents when you were born?

   _____

IT'S YOUR BIRTHDAY!

"A child needs a grandparent, anybody's grandparent, to grow a
little more securely into an unfamiliar world." — Charles and Ann Morse

8. What was your height (length) and weight at birth?

_____

9. Were you the oldest, middle, or youngest child? How
   many siblings do you have?

_____

_____

10. What have your parents told you about how you were
    as a baby?

_____

_____

_____

_____

_____

_____

_____

_____

_____

_____

IT'S YOUR BIRTHDAY!

"Love is the greatest gift that one generation
can leave to another."— Richard Garnett

11. What stories have you been told about the day you
were born?

_____

_____

_____

_____

_____

_____

_____

_____

_____

_____

_____

_____

_____

_____

_____

IT'S YOUR BIRTHDAY!
"When grandparents enter the door, discipline
flies out the window." — Ogden Nash

12. What is your earliest childhood memory?

_____

_____

_____

_____

_____

_____

_____

_____

_____

_____

_____

_____

FAMILY TREE

"A grandfather is someone with silver in
his hair and gold in his heart." — Author Unknown

My Mother's Great-
Grandmother

My Mother's Great-
Grandfather

My Mother's
Grandmother

My Mother's
Grandfather

My Mother's Mother

My Mother's Father

My Mother

FAMILY TREE

"Every generation revolts against its fathers and
makes friends with its grandfathers." — Lewis Mumford

My Father's Great-
Grandmother

My Father's Great-
Grandfather

My Father's
Grandmother

My Father's
Grandfather

My Father's Mother

My Father's Father

My Father

GROWING UP

"Grandfathers are for loving and fixing things." —Author Unknown

1. Where did you live in your elementary school years?

_____

_____

_____

2. Did you have a nickname?

_____

3. What was your favorite treat when you were a kid?

_____

_____

_____

4. What were your regular chores?

_____

_____

_____

_____

5. Did you get an allowance? If yes, how much?

_____

_____

GROWING UP

"Grandfathers are just antique little boys." — Author Unknown

6. Who was your best friend?

_____

_____

7. What did you do on a typical Saturday when you were a kid?

_____

_____

_____

_____

_____

_____

8. What do you miss most about being a kid?

_____

_____

_____

_____

_____

_____

GROWING UP

"Even though you're growing up, you
should never stop having fun." — Nina Dobrev

9. Describe what you were like when you were a kid.

_____

_____

_____

_____

_____

_____

_____

10. What was the worst trouble you remember getting into
    as a kid?

_____

_____

_____

_____

_____

_____

_____

WHERE HAVE YOU LIVED?

"Grandpa has ears that truly listen, arms that always hold, love that's never ending and a heart that's made of gold." — Author Unknown

List the cities you have lived in during your life. Include the dates if you can remember them.

_____

_____

_____

_____

_____

_____

_____

_____

_____

_____

_____

_____

_____

_____

THE TEENAGE YEARS

"A baby has a way of making a man out of his father
and a boy out of his grandfather." — Angie Papadakis

1. How did you dress and style your hair during your teens?
   Do you have any pictures?

   _____

   _____

   _____

   _____

   _____

2. Did you hang out with a group of people or a few close
   friends? Do you still talk to any of them?

   _____

   _____

   _____

   _____

3. In what kind of car did you learn to drive?

   _____

   _____

4. Who taught you to drive?

   _____

   _____

THE TEENAGE YEARS

"My grandfather was a wonderful role model. Through
him I got to know the gentle side of men." — Sarah Long

5. Did you have a girlfriend in high school? Did you have
   any serious relationships in your teen years?

   _____

   _____

   _____

6. Did you have a curfew?

   _____

   _____

7. Did you ever get in trouble for missing your curfew?
   What was your punishment?

   _____

   _____

   _____

   _____

8. Did you go to any school dances? What were they like?

   _____

   _____

   _____

   _____

THE TEENAGE YEARS

"Beautiful young people are accidents of nature. But beautiful old people are works of art." — Marjory Barslow-Greenbie

9. What was a common weekend night like during your teens?

_____

_____

_____

_____

_____

10. Knowing all you know now, what advice would you give your teenage self?

_____

_____

_____

_____

_____

_____

_____

_____

THE TEENAGE YEARS
"Having a teenager can cause parents to
wonder about each other's heredity." — Unknown

11. Describe what you were like during your teen years.

_____

_____

_____

_____

_____

_____

_____

12. Write about a favorite memory from your teens.

_____

_____

_____

_____

_____

_____

_____

WHAT HAPPENED THE YEAR YOU WERE BORN?

"One of the most powerful handclasps is that of a new grandbaby around the finger of a grandfather." —Joy Hargrove

Google the following for the year you were born:

1. What historical events occurred?

_____

_____

_____

_____

2. What movie won the Academy Award for Best Picture? Who won Best Actor and Best Actress?

_____

_____

_____

_____

3. What were a few popular movies that came out the year you were born?

_____

_____

_____

_____

WHAT HAPPENED THE YEAR YOU WERE BORN?

"Grandparents make the world ... a little softer,
a little kinder, a little warmer." —Unknown

4. What song was on the top of the Billboard charts?

_____

5. Who was the President of the United States?

_____

6. What were a few popular television or radio shows?

_____

_____

_____

_____

_____

7. What were the prices for the following items?
- A loaf of bread:
- A gallon of milk:
- A cup of coffee:
- A dozen eggs:
- The average cost of a new home:
- A first-class stamp:
- A new car:
- A gallon of gas:
- A movie ticket:

"Great fathers get promoted to grandfathers."
– Unknown

"My grandfather's words are always in my ear and his heart is always my guide'."
- Unknown

WHAT KIND OF STUDENT WERE YOU?

"You've got to do your own growing, no matter how tall your grandfather was." — Abraham Lincoln

1. What did you like and dislike about school?

   _____

   _____

   _____

   _____

2. What kind of grades did you get?

   _____

   _____

3. What were your favorite and least favorite subjects?

   _____

   _____

4. What was your relationship with your parents like during your high school years?

   _____

   _____

   _____

   _____

WHAT KIND OF STUDENT WERE YOU?

"More and more, when I single out the person out who inspired me most, I go back to my grandfather." — James Earl Jones

5. Did you play any sports?

_____

_____

6. What were the school activities that you took part in?

_____

_____

_____

7. Is there a teacher or coach that had a significant impact on you? What was their biggest influence?

_____

_____

_____

_____

_____

_____

_____

_____

WHAT KIND OF STUDENT WERE YOU?

"We don't stop going to school when we graduate."
— Carol Burnett

8. What were a few of your favorite songs from your high school years?

_____

_____

_____

_____

_____

9. What would you have done differently in school if you knew then what you know now?

_____

_____

_____

_____

_____

_____

_____

_____

WHAT KIND OF STUDENT WERE YOU?

"Education is what remains after one has forgotten what one has learned in school." — Albert Einstein

10. Write about a favorite memory from your high school years.

_____

_____

_____

_____

_____

_____

_____

_____

_____

_____

_____

_____

_____

_____

_____

_____

_____

GRANDFATHER TRIVIA

"A grandfather is someone you can look up to
no matter how tall you grow." — Author Unknown

1. What is your favorite flavor of ice cream?

   _____

2. How do you like your coffee?

   _____

3. How do you like your eggs cooked?

   _____

4. If money were not a concern, where would you want to live?

   _____

   _____

5. Do you still have your tonsils?

   _____

6. What is your shoe size?

   _____

7. How old were you when you started to walk?

   _____

8. Do you have any allergies?

   _____

   _____

   _____

GRANDFATHER TRIVIA

"Nobody can do for little children what grandparents do. Grandparents sort of sprinkle stardust over the lives of little children." —Alex Haley

9. What is the eye color of each of your kids?

_____

_____

_____

_____

_____

10. What superpower would you pick for yourself?

_____

_____

11. What would you pick as your last meal?

_____

_____

_____

_____

12. Preference: cook or clean?

_____

13. Were you a Boy Scout?

_____

YOUR PARENTS

"Grandpas bring a little wisdom, happiness, warmth, and love to every life they touch." – Author Unknown

1. Where was your mother born and where did she grow up?

   _____

   _____

   _____

   _____

2. What three words would you use to describe her?

   _____

   _____

3. In what ways are you most like your mother?

   _____

   _____

   _____

   _____

   _____

   _____

   _____

YOUR PARENTS

"Only the best dads get promoted to grandpa."
— Author Unknown

4. Where was your father born and where did he grow up?

_____

_____

_____

5. What three words would you use to describe him?

_____

_____

_____

6. In what ways are you like your father?

_____

_____

_____

_____

_____

_____

_____

_____

YOUR PARENTS
"Grandparents are the best kind of grownups."
— Unknown

7. How did your parents meet?

_____

_____

_____

_____

_____

8. Describe your parent's relationship.

_____

_____

_____

_____

_____

_____

9. Did either of them have any unique talents?

_____

_____

_____

_____

YOUR PARENTS

"Grandpa has ears that truly listen, arms that always hold, love that's never-ending, and a heart that's made of gold." —Author Unknown

10. Do we have any family traditions that come from your parents or grandparents?

_____

_____

_____

_____

_____

11. What were your parent's occupations?

_____

_____

_____

12. What other individuals had a major role in helping you grow up? What were their biggest influences?

_____

_____

_____

_____

_____

_____

"My grandfather
once told me
that there were
two kinds of people:
those who do
the work and
those who take the
credit.
He told me to try
to be in the first group;
there was much less
competition."
—Indira Gandhi

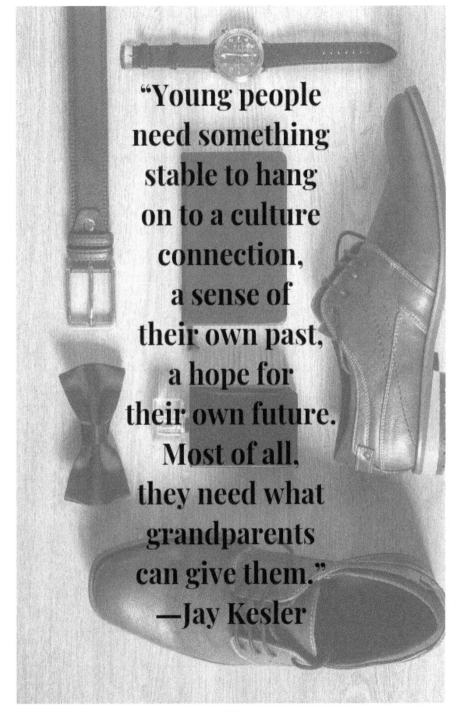

"Young people need something stable to hang on to a culture connection, a sense of their own past, a hope for their own future. Most of all, they need what grandparents can give them."
—Jay Kesler

BECOMING A DAD

"A father is a man who expects his children
to be as good as he meant to be." — Carol Coats

1. How old were you when you first became a father?

   _____

2. Who was the first person you told that you were going
   to be a dad?

   _____

   _____

   _____

3. Is there a specific song you would sing or play to your
   kids when they were little?

   _____

   _____

   _____

4. What is the biggest difference in how kids are raised
   today than when you were a kid?

   _____

   _____

   _____

   _____

   _____

BECOMING A DAD

"Grandfathers give us not only wisdom and encouragement,
but they are an inspiration to us." — Kate Summers

5. What are the ways you would change about how your kids were raised?

_____

_____

_____

_____

_____

_____

6. Knowing what you know now, what advice would you give yourself as a new father?

_____

_____

_____

_____

_____

_____

_____

BECOMING A DAD

"Grandparents are there to help the child get into mischief they haven't thought of yet." —Gene Perret

7. What is the best and hardest parts about being a father?

_____

_____

_____

_____

_____

_____

_____

_____

_____

_____

_____

_____

_____

BECOMING A DAD

"Being a great father is like shaving. No matter how good
you shaved today, you have to do it again tomorrow."
— Reed Markham

8. Write about a favorite memory of being a father.

_____

_____

_____

_____

_____

_____

_____

_____

_____

_____

_____

_____

_____

_____

SPIRITUALITY & RELIGION

"Sometimes our grandmas and grandpas
are like grand-angels." — Lexie Saige

1. Were your parents religious when you were growing up?

_____

2. How did your parents express their spiritual beliefs?

_____

_____

_____

_____

3. What role does religion have in your life?

_____

_____

_____

_____

4. Do you believe in miracles? Have you experienced one?

_____

_____

_____

_____

SPIRITUALITY & RELIGION

"There are only two ways to live your life. One is as though nothing is a miracle.
The other is as though everything is a miracle." — Albert Einstein

5. What do you have faith in?

_____

_____

_____

_____

_____

6. Do you pray? If yes, how often and to whom do you pray?

_____

_____

_____

7. How have your religious beliefs and practices changed over the course of your life?

_____

_____

_____

_____

_____

_____

SPIRITUALITY & RELIGION

"Within you there is a stillness and a sanctuary to which you
can retreat at any time and be yourself." — Hermann Hesse

8. What is your current religious or spiritual practice?

_____

_____

_____

_____

_____

_____

_____

9. Which do you think has the most impact on our lives:
   fate or free will? Why do you feel this way?

_____

_____

_____

_____

_____

_____

SPIRITUALITY & RELIGION

"Nothing is, unless our thinking makes it so."
— William Shakespeare

10. What do you think is the purpose of life?

_____

_____

_____

_____

_____

_____

_____

11. What do you do in moments when times are challenging, and you need inner strength?

_____

_____

_____

_____

_____

_____

WORK & CAREER

"A grandfather has the wisdom of long experience
and the love of an understanding heart." —Author Unknown

1. When you were a kid, what did you want to be when you grew up?

   _____

   _____

2. What was your first job?

   _____

   _____

3. How many jobs have you had during your lifetime? List a few of your favorites.

   _____

   _____

   _____

   _____

4. What are the favorite and least favorite jobs you have had?

   _____

   _____

   _____

   _____

WORK & CAREER

"Grandchildren are the dots that connect the
lines from generation to generation." —Lois Wyse

5. Have you ever wanted to have your own business? If
   yes, what kind of business would it be?

   _____

   _____

   _____

6. What are three jobs you would never want to have?

   _____

   _____

   _____

7. Is there a job or profession your parents wanted you to
   pursue? If yes, what was it?

   _____

   _____

   _____

8. If you could do any profession, what would it be?

   _____

   _____

   _____

   _____

"Our land
is everything to us....
I will tell you
one of the things
we remember
on our land.
We remember
that our grandfathers
paid for it
— with their lives."
—John Wooden

"Grandchildren
don't stay
young forever,
which is good
because grandfathers
only have
so many horsy rides
in them."
—Author Unknown

LOVE & ROMANCE

"The reason grandchildren and grandparents get along so
well is that they have a common enemy." — Sam Levenson

1. What was the biggest crush you had when you were in
   high school?

   _____

   _____

   _____

2. What age were you when you had your first date?

   _____

   _____

   _____

3. Who was it with and what did you do?

   _____

   _____

   _____

   _____

4. How old were you when you had your first kiss?

   _____

5. Do you believe in love at first sight?

   _____

LOVE & ROMANCE

"What a bargain grandchildren are! I give them my loose change,
and they give me a million dollars' worth of pleasure." — Gene Perret

6. Do you believe in soul mates?

_____

7. Have you ever written someone a love poem or song?

_____

8. If yes, write a few lines that you may remember.

_____

_____

_____

_____

_____

9. What is your most romantic memory?

_____

_____

_____

_____

_____

_____

LOVE & ROMANCE

"You know you're in love when you can't fall asleep
because reality is finally better than your dreams." — Dr. Seuss

10. What is your opinion of online dating?

_____

_____

_____

11. In your opinion, what are the most important qualities
of a successful relationship?

_____

_____

_____

_____

_____

12. What is the biggest way relationships have changed
over the years?

_____

_____

_____

_____

_____

LOVE & ROMANCE

"It is not a lack of love, but a lack of friendship
that makes unhappy marriages." — Friedrich Nietzsche

13. Write about a time you experienced a broken heart.
How did you get over it?

_____

_____

_____

_____

_____

_____

_____

_____

_____

_____

_____

_____

_____

_____

_____

_____

POLITICAL STUFF

"My grandfather did a lot of things in his life. What he
was most proud of was raising his family." — Tagg Romney

1. How old were you when you voted for the first time?

   _____

2. When was the last time you voted?

   _____

3. How have your political opinions changed over the
   years?

   _____

   _____

   _____

   _____

   _____

   _____

   _____

4. What do you think are the three most serious issues
   facing our country?

   _____

   _____

   _____

POLITICAL STUFF
"Happiness is a grandpa hug." —Gene Perret

5. Have you ever participated in a march, protest, or boycott? If no, what issue could motivate you to join?

_____

_____

_____

6. Who in your family would you guess votes differently than you?

_____

_____

_____

_____

7. Who is your favorite political or historical figure? Why do you admire them?

_____

_____

_____

_____

_____

_____

POLITICAL STUFF

"Politics, it seems to me, has been concerned with
right or left instead of right or wrong." — Richard Armour

8. What are the positive and negative impacts your
generation has had on the country and the world?

_____

_____

_____

_____

_____

_____

9. In what ways do you agree and disagree with the
political choices of your children's generation.

_____

_____

_____

_____

_____

_____

_____

POLITICAL STUFF

"In politics stupidity is not a handicap."
— Napoleon Bonaparte

10. Who is the best president of your lifetime?

_____

11. If you woke up tomorrow and found yourself in charge of the entire country, what are the first five things would you enact or change?

One:

_____

_____

Two:

_____

_____

Three:

_____

_____

Four:

_____

_____

Five:

_____

_____

GRANDFATHER TRIVIA

"Grandchildren are God's way of compensating
us for growing old." — Mary H. Waldrip

1. Do you read your horoscope?

   _____

2. What motivates you?

   _____

   _____

   _____

   _____

3. What is your biggest big pet peeve?

   _____

4. Do you ever buy lottery tickets?

   _____

5. What is your favorite season of the year?

   _____

6. If you could do any one thing for a whole day, what
   would it be?

   _____

   _____

7. Have you ever fired a gun?

   _____

GRANDFATHER TRIVIA

"The best place to be when you're sad is Grandpa's lap."
—Author Unknown

8. Who is your hero? Why?

_____

_____

_____

_____

9. If you could only eat three things for the next year, with no harm to your health, what would they be?

_____

_____

_____

10. What can you do better than anyone else in the family?

_____

_____

_____

11. What were the names of your childhood pets?

_____

_____

_____

"To a small child,
the perfect granddad
is unafraid
of big dogs
and fierce storms
but absolutely
terrified of
the word "boo."
—Robert Brault

"You don't
choose
your family.
They are God's gift
to you, as you
are to them."
—Desmond Tutu

LET'S TALK ABOUT YOUR KIDS

"Grandpa has ears that truly listen, arms that always hold, love that's never-ending, and a heart that's made of gold." —Author Unknown

1. What would your kids' names be if they had been born the opposite gender?

_____

_____

_____

_____

2. Who did your children most look like when they were babies?

_____

_____

_____

_____

3. What were your kids' first words?

_____

_____

_____

_____

LET'S TALK ABOUT YOUR KIDS

"To be able to watch your children's children grow up is truly a blessing from above." — Byron Pulsifer

4. How old were they when they took their first step?

_____

_____

_____

_____

5. How many of your children were planned and how many were "surprises?"

_____

_____

6. Is there a specific book you remember reading to your kids?

_____

_____

7. When your kids were babies, what trick did you use to calm them when they were upset?

_____

_____

_____

_____

LET'S TALK ABOUT YOUR KIDS

"Adults are just outdated children." — Dr. Seuss

8. What is your first memory of each of your children?

_____

_____

_____

_____

_____

_____

_____

_____

_____

_____

_____

_____

_____

LET'S TALK ABOUT YOUR KIDS
"Children are a poor man's riches." — English Proverb

9. In what ways are your kids like you and how are they different?

_____

_____

_____

_____

_____

_____

_____

_____

_____

_____

_____

_____

_____

_____

_____

LET'S TALK ABOUT YOUR GRANDKIDS

"Grandparents are a delightful blend of laughter, caring deeds, wonderful stories, and love." — Author Unknown

1. How old were you when you first became a grandfather?

_____

_____

2. How many grandkids do you have?

_____

_____

3. How were you told that you would be a grandfather? What was your reaction when you heard the news?

_____

_____

_____

_____

4. What do you remember about the first time you held your first grandchild?

_____

_____

_____

_____

LET'S TALK ABOUT YOUR GRANDKIDS

"Unconditional positive regard is rarely given
by anyone except a grandparent." — Unknown

5. What are your grandkids' nicknames?

_____

_____

6. How is being a grandfather different than being a father?

_____

_____

_____

_____

_____

7. What is the most surprising thing about being a grandfather?

_____

_____

_____

_____

TRAVEL

"One's destination is never a place, but a
new way of seeing things." — Henry Miller

1. Do you have a valid passport?

_____

2. What is your fantasy vacation?

_____

_____

_____

_____

3. Are you a light or heavy packer?

_____

4. What is the one thing from home you always bring with
   you on a trip?

_____

_____

_____

5. When traveling, do you stick to familiar foods or do
   you look for places where the locals eat?

_____

_____

_____

TRAVEL

"A mind that is stretched by a new experience can never go back to its old dimensions." — Oliver Wendell Holmes

6. What is your favorite travel memory?

_____

_____

_____

_____

_____

_____

_____

_____

7. Write about a travel memory from when you were a kid.

_____

_____

_____

_____

_____

_____

TRAVEL BUCKET LIST

"Life is short, and the world is wide." — Unknown

List the top 10 places you would visit if money and time were no concern. Write about why for each choice.

1. _____

_____

2. _____

_____

3. _____

_____

4. _____

_____

5. _____

_____

TRAVEL BUCKET LIST

"Travel makes one modest, you see what a tiny place you
occupy in the world." — Gustave Flaubert

Continued

6. _____

_____

7. _____

_____

8. _____

_____

9. _____

_____

10. _____

_____

"Grandchildren
give us a
second chance
to do things
better because
they bring
out the
best in us."
—Author Unknown

"Our grandchildren accept us for ourselves, without rebuke or effort to change us, as no one in our entire lives has ever done, not our parents, siblings, spouses, friends — and hardly ever our own grown children."
—Ruth Goode

MEMORIES

"Memory is a way of holding on to the things you love, the things you are, the things you never want to lose." — Unknown

What is a favorite memory of your Mother?

_____

_____

_____

_____

_____

_____

_____

_____

_____

_____

_____

_____

_____

MEMORIES

"We don't remember days, we remember moments."
— Unknown

What is a favorite memory of your Father?

_____

_____

_____

_____

_____

_____

_____

_____

_____

_____

_____

_____

_____

_____

_____

SPORTS MEMORIES

"My grandfather always said that living is like
licking honey off a thorn." — Louis Adamic

1. When you were a kid, did you ever think about being a
   professional athlete? Which sport?

   _____

   _____

2. Growing up, what was your favorite sport? Did you
   have a favorite team?

   _____

   _____

   _____

3. Who is your favorite player of all time in any sport?

   _____

   _____

   _____

   _____

4. If money and time was no object, what sporting event
   do you most want to attend?

   _____

   _____

   _____

   _____

SPORTS MEMORIES

"If I had known how wonderful it would be to have grandchildren, I'd have had them first." —Lois Wyse

5. What was the first professional sporting event you attended in person?

_____

_____

6. What was the most crushing defeat you experienced playing or watching a sporting event?

_____

_____

_____

_____

_____

7. Is there a sporting event you saw as a kid that you still vividly remember?

_____

_____

_____

_____

8. What is your favorite sports movie?

_____

_____

GRANDFATHER TRIVIA

"I have found the best way to give advice to your children
is to find out what they want and then advise them to do it."
— Harry S. Truman

1. What would be the title of your autobiography?

_____

_____

_____

2. Do you think you could still pass the written portion
   of the driver's test without studying?

_____

3. What is your favorite line from a movie?

_____

_____

_____

4. Do you believe in life on other planets?

_____

_____

5. If you were forced to sing karaoke, what song would
   you pick to perform?

_____

_____

_____

GRANDFATHER TRIVIA

"When I was a kid, my parents moved a lot,
but I always found them." — Rodney Dangerfield

6. What is your favorite color?

_____

7. What is the first movie you can remember seeing?

_____

_____

8. Who was your role model growing up? What impact did they have on you?

_____

_____

_____

_____

_____

_____

9. When was the last time a movie or something on television made you cry? What was it?

_____

_____

_____

ADVICE

"Sometimes the poorest man leaves his children
the richest inheritance." — Ruth E. Renkel

What was the best advice your mother gave you?

_____

_____

_____

_____

_____

_____

_____

What was the best advice your father gave you?

_____

_____

_____

_____

_____

_____

_____

_____

ADVICE

"Children are likely to live up to what you believe of them."
— Lady Bird Johnson

Based upon what you have learned and what you have experienced, what is the one key piece of advice you would give your children?

_____

_____

_____

_____

_____

_____

_____

_____

_____

_____

_____

_____

_____

QUESTIONS

"Everyone needs to have access both to grandparents and
grandchildren in order to be a full human being." — Margaret Mead

What is the question you have you always wanted to
ask your parents?

_____

_____

_____

_____

_____

_____

What question would you like your kids to ask you?

_____

_____

_____

_____

_____

_____

_____

_____

QUESTIONS

"The smart, kind, beautiful child... must have
got it from their grandparents." — Unknown

How would you like to be remembered by your family
and friends?

_____

_____

_____

_____

_____

_____

_____

_____

_____

_____

_____

_____

_____

_____

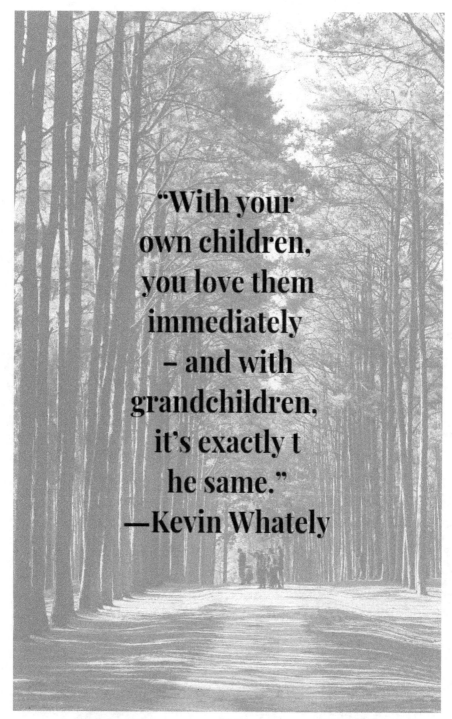

"With your own children, you love them immediately – and with grandchildren, it's exactly t he same."
—Kevin Whately

"Grandfathers do have a special place in the lives of their children's children. They can delight and play with them and even indulge them in ways that they did not indulge their own children. Grandfather knows that after the fun and games are over with his adorable grandchildren he can return to the quiet of his own home and peacefully reflect on this phenomenon of fatherhood."
—Alvin Poussaint

MOVIES, MUSIC, TELEVISION, & BOOKS

"What a bargain grandchildren are! I give them my loose change, and they give me a million dollars' worth of pleasure."
— Gene Perret

1. What movie do you think you have watched the highest number of times?

_____

_____

2. What is a movie you can remember loving when you were a kid?

_____

_____

_____

3. Who would you cast to play yourself in the movie of your life? How about the rest of your family?

_____

_____

_____

_____

_____

_____

MOVIES, MUSIC, TELEVISION, & BOOKS

"I was taught by my grandfather that anything that your mind can conceive, you can have. It's a reality." —Lenny Kravitz

4. What are your favorite genres of music?

_____

_____

_____

_____

5. Which decades had the best music?

_____

_____

_____

_____

6. What is the first record, album, cassette, or tape you remember buying?

_____

_____

7. Name a song that you like today that would make your younger self cringe?

_____

_____

MOVIES, MUSIC, TELEVISION, & BOOKS

"Grandpas always have time for you when
everyone else is too busy. — Unknown

8. What was the first concert you attended? What year was
    it?

    _____

    _____

    _____

9. In what ways has your taste in music changed over the
    years?

    _____

    _____

    _____

    _____

    _____

10. What is the first song you can remember loving?

    _____

    _____

11. If you had to pick a theme song for your life, what song
    would you pick?

    _____

    _____

MOVIES, MUSIC, TELEVISION, & BOOKS

"My grandfather taught me how important it is to have your eyes open, because you never know what's going to come your way." —Bobbi Brown

12. What television show from the past do you wish was still on the air?

_____

_____

13. If you could be on any television show or movie, past or present, which one would you pick?

_____

_____

14. What is a favorite book from your childhood or teen years?

_____

_____

15. What book or books have positively impacted the way you think, work, or live your life?

_____

_____

_____

_____

TOP TEN MOVIES

"All grandfathers possess a limitless amount of interesting stories gathered from the past." —Author Unknown

List Your Ten Favorite Movies:

1. _____

   _____

2. _____

   _____

3. _____

   _____

4. _____

   _____

5. _____

   _____

6. _____

   _____

7. _____

   _____

8. _____

   _____

9. _____

   _____

10. _____

TOP TEN SONGS

"Perfect love sometimes does not come till the first
grandchild." — Welsh Proverb

List Your Ten Favorite Songs:

11. _____

_____

12. _____

_____

13. _____

_____

14. _____

_____

15. _____

_____

16. _____

_____

17. _____

_____

18. _____

_____

19. _____

_____

20. _____

GRANDFATHER TRIVIA

"Grandparents, like heroes, are as necessary to a child's growth as vitamins." — Joyce Allston

1. How many speeding tickets have you received?

   _____

2. What is your favorite holiday?

   _____

3. If you could have dinner with any five people who have ever lived, who would you pick?

   _____

   _____

   _____

   _____

   _____

4. What bones have you broken?

   _____

   _____

   _____

   _____

5. What is your dream car?

   _____

GRANDFATHER TRIVIA
"Grandparents are a treasure in the family."
— Pope Francis

6. What accomplishment are you most proud of yourself for achieving?

_____

_____

_____

_____

7. Is there anything in your family's medical history that your kids should know about?

_____

_____

_____

_____

8. What is your favorite thing about yourself?

_____

_____

_____

_____

_____

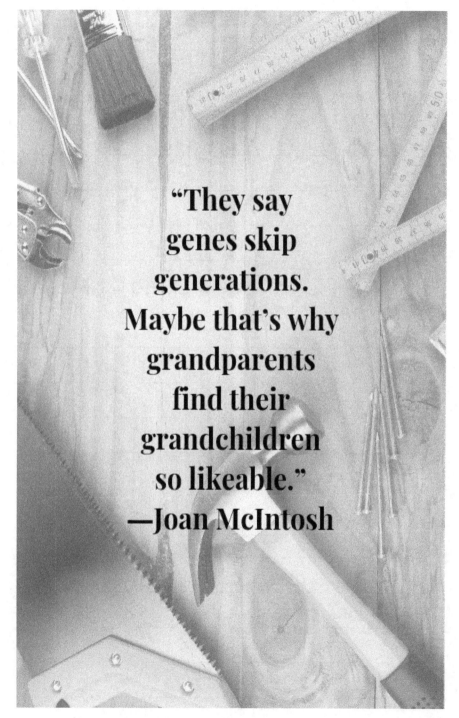

"They say genes skip generations. Maybe that's why grandparents find their grandchildren so likeable."
—Joan McIntosh

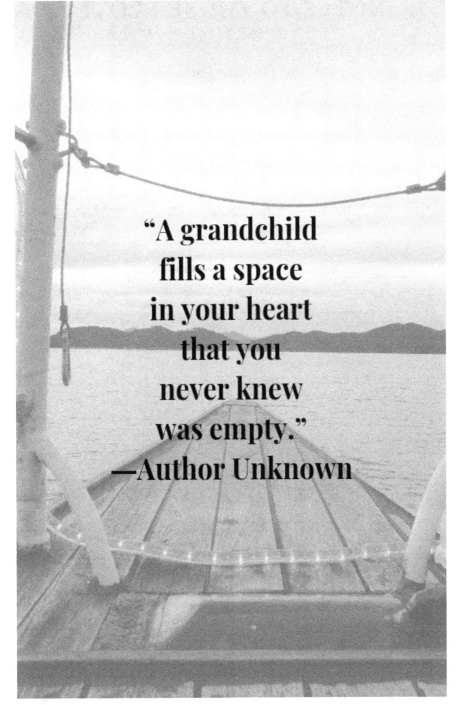

"A grandchild
fills a space
in your heart
that you
never knew
was empty."
—Author Unknown

NOTES TO THOSE I LOVE
"Letters mingle souls." — Unknown

This is space for you to write notes to your family.

_____

_____

_____

_____

_____

_____

_____

_____

_____

_____

_____

_____

_____

_____

_____

_____

NOTES TO THOSE I LOVE

"Letters are among the most significant memorial a person can leave behind them." — Johann Wolfgang von Goethe

This is space for you to write notes to your family.

_____

_____

_____

_____

_____

_____

_____

_____

_____

_____

_____

_____

_____

_____

NOTES TO THOSE I LOVE

"The only thing most people do better than anyone
else is read their own handwriting." — John Adams

This is space for you to write notes to your family.

_____

_____

_____

_____

_____

_____

_____

_____

_____

_____

_____

_____

_____

NOTES TO THOSE I LOVE

"After a good dinner one can forgive anybody, even one's own relations." — Oscar Wilde, A Woman of No Importance

This is space for you to write notes to your family.

_____

_____

_____

_____

_____

_____

_____

_____

_____

_____

_____

_____

_____

_____

NOTES TO THOSE I LOVE
"A happy family is but an earlier heaven."
— George Bernard Shaw

This is space for you to write notes to your family.

_____

_____

_____

_____

_____

_____

_____

_____

_____

_____

_____

_____

NOTES TO THOSE I LOVE

"The greatest gifts you can give your children are the roots of responsibility and the wings of independence." — Denis Waitley

This is space for you to write notes to your family.

_____

_____

_____

_____

_____

_____

_____

_____

_____

_____

_____

_____

_____

About the Author

Jeffrey Mason has spent twenty-plus years working with individuals, couples, and organizations helping them to create change, achieve goals, and strengthen their relationships.

He begins with the understanding that being human is hard and is committed to helping others understand that forgiveness is the greatest gift we can give others and ourselves.

Jeffrey would be grateful if you would help people find his books by leaving a review on Amazon. Your feedback helps him get better at this thing he loves.

You can contact him at hello@jeffreymason.com, www.jeffreymason.com, or hearyourstory.com. He would love to hear from you.

The Hear Your Story Line of Books

At **Hear Your Story**, we have created a line of books focused on giving each of us a place to tell the unique story of who we are, where we have been, and where we are going.

Sharing and hearing the stories of the people in our lives creates communication, closeness, understanding, and the cement of a forever bond.

- Dad, I Want to Hear Your Story; A Father's Guided Journal to Share His Life & His Love

- Mom, I Want to Hear Your Story; A Mother's Guided Journal to Share Her Life & Her Love

- You Chose to Be My Dad; I Want to Hear Your Story: A Guided Journal for Stepdads to Share Their Life Story

- Life Gave Me You; I Want to Hear Your Story: A Guided Journal for Stepmothers to Share Their Life Story

The Hear Your Story Line of Books

- Grandmother, I Want to Hear Your Story: A Grandmother's Guided Journal to Share Her Life and Her Love

- Grandfather, I Want to Hear Your Story: A Grandfather's Guided Journal to Share His Life and His Love

- Dad Notes: Dad, I Wrote This Book for You

- Mom Notes: I Wrote This Book About the Best Mother Ever

- Because I Love You: The Couple's Bucket List That Builds Your Relationship

- Love Notes: I Wrote This Book About You

- Our Story: A Couple's Guided Journal

- You, Me, and Us: 229 Fun Relationship Questions to Ask Your Guy or Girl

- Papá, quiero oír tu historia: El diario guiado de un padre Para compartir su vida y su amor

Available at Amazon and all Bookstores

You can view and answer the questions in this book at www.hearyourstory.com. Access can be through any computer, tablet, or smartphone.

This website gives you the capability to answer the questions and then print multiple copies of your responses to give to your entire family.

Please note there is a small charge to cover the cost of maintaining the site

To My Grandfathers
Claude Mason & Joseph Niles

My Grandfathers were men of their time.

They were men who never got to be boys. Their work lives began at early ages and they had jobs that were hard on the body.

They did what they could with what they had, and did it for paychecks that was often gone before it arrived.

Granddaddy Mason, I have so many things that come to mind when I think of you. Eighteen wheelers, CB radios, crackers in your milk, Copenhagen, a patch covered eye. Mostly I remember your stores.

You had so many! You would sit in your chair with your spit can close by and you would tell tales of driving trucks and the war and growing up and anything else that came to your mind.

You told stories. Your Son, My Dad, told stories. I tell stories. My kids tell stories. This is who we are, and this is the constant that connects us.

Granddaddy Niles, I am told I met you when I was little. I was young, so my memory doesn't have a home for that time. I do have Mom's mentions in occasional wistful bursts, a proud picture of you on my shelf, and the knowing that I am because you are.

To my grandfathers: we are linked in life and legacy, blood, and tradition. You are forever, planted in your yesterdays and my kids' tomorrows. Thank you to both of you.

CPSIA information can be obtained
at www.ICGtesting.com
Printed in the USA
BVHW061427210622
640288BV00003B/232